POEMS: *A Selection*

POEMS

A SELECTION

LÉONIE ADAMS

FUNK & WAGNALLS

COMPANY

NEW YORK · 1954 ·

ACKNOWLEDGMENT

The following poems in Section II of this book are from *Those Not Elect*, copyright 1925 and 1953, by Léonie Adams, Robert M. McBride and Company, New York:

Those Not Elect, Quiet, Thought's End, A Wind of Fall, April Mortality, An Old Spell, Spire of Saint Patrick's and the Moon, Homecoming, Merry Month of May, Midsummer, A Gull Goes Up, Death and the Lady, Bird and Bosom — Apocalyptic, Prelude Pastoral, Discourse with the Heart, Thief of Paradise, Companions of the Morass, Pity of the Heavens, Said of the Earth and the Moon, Night of Unshed Tears, The Barouche, At Tea One Bitter Afternoon, To the Waterfront Pigeons, Twilight of the Wood.

The other poems in Section II are selected from *High Falcon* by Léonie Adams, copyright 1929 by Léonie Adams, The John Day Company, Inc., New York.

Second Printing

POEMS: A SELECTION

LIBRARY OF CONGRESS CATALOG CARD NUMBER 54-6356

PRINTED IN THE UNITED STATES OF AMERICA

To *William Troy*

I: Fruits of Two Seasons

II: As Apt Was Joy

POEMS: *A Selection*

I: *Fruits of Two Seasons*

The child's toys and the old man's reasons
Are the fruits of the two seasons.
WILLIAM BLAKE

Birds are of passage now,
Else-wending; where—
Songless, soon gone of late—
They night among us,
No tone now upon grass
Downcast from hedge or grove
With goldening day invites.
Cold, wizening, drear
Lies there all shadowing over.
Yet some, then many from
The blanched net flit and call,
Still a time gambolling;
Into, from the numb skein,
Two, a third with least tune;
And one on the sunned end
Of lawn turns and turns,
With rime-bedabbled wing.

Air as of two airs
Through day lifts and plays,
In a day that looks away,
Bloom-dappling in the cleft
Of the stone distances,
And the dimmed forest weft;
And in reddish hues upshed
From about autumnal things
Shines tenderer, afar seen,
Lastingly after-lit,
Out of all seasons spring;
In a day that looks far,

A day that sees plain,
Roseate at feet the fresh
Fall of leaf we rake upon
The fallen mouldered brown;
That infiltrate of light,
Lace then the day pours through,
And the winged seed down-lain.

Clime of two climes
Seems here in time straying,
Its whisperer within sun,
Where in warm musing is stood;
And light to the cheek of flesh
All without sifts cool
Upon the sun-warmed one.
Nearer eared than the heard,
The silences beneath
Of pathos without cry.
In sight fulfilling the eyes,
Vistaed of the beheld
Are its beseechings; wide
Those intimations whence,
Only its offering offering,
Climbs then an eyebeam
To its endless portion;
As it were a vista upon
The suffered and foredone.

Grapes Making

Noon sun beats down the leaf; the noon
Of summer burns along the vine
And thins the leaf with burning air,
Till from the underleaf is fanned,
And down the woven vine, the light.
Still the pleached leaves drop layer on layer
To wind the sun on either hand,
And echoes of the light are bound,
And hushed the blazing cheek of light,
The hurry of the breathless noon,
And from the thicket of the vine
The grape has pressed into its round.

The grape has pressed into its round,
And swings, aloof chill green, clean won
Of light, between the sky and ground;
Those hid, soft-flashing lamps yet blind,
Which yield an apprehended sun.
Fresh triumph in a courteous kind,
Having more ways to be, and years,
And easy, countless treasuries,
You whose all-told is still no sum,
Like a rich heart, well-said in sighs,
The careless autumn mornings come,
The grapes drop glimmering to the shears.

Now shady sod at heel piles deep,
An overarching shade, the vine
Across the fall of noon is flung;
And here beneath the leaves is cast

A light to colour noonday sleep,
While cool, bemused the grape is swung
Beneath the eyelids of the vine;
And deepening like a tender thought
Green moves along the leaf, and bright
The leaf above, and leaf has caught,
And emerald pierces day, and last
The faint leaf vanishes to light.

When Green

When green swept up the cold turfside,
And boughs unbosomed May,
An old man's step was on this orchard ground,
That asked of each green inch its way;
While one at his hand trod,
For pride and will within her then,
As to upbear the sod.

The new graft prospers on old stock,
Though who knows how an orchard branch will teach
Its winter edge with whisperings of the sap,
Or an old man in speech?
And this alone was new to the ear of youth:
An accent rheum-beset, which broke to give
Its innocent names for truth.

Griefs which waste from the bone he left unsaid,
And chances to befall a callow breast;
His speech was words from a speller, stories
Of the favoured of time at rest,
While green went up in tide,
And his step sought its way of earth,
The light footfall beside.

Nightpiece

The moon above the milky field
Gleaning moves her one slant light;
Wind weeps from out its cloud.
Then, weeping wind, unshroud
Pale Cassiopeia, blow
The true-swung pole-lamp bright:
To this room a midnight's come
That speaks but with the beating clock,
While on glistening paws the mouse
Creeps nightmaster of the house.
Rust shall eat away the lock,
The door sag from the garner-hoard,
And the sleeper lie unsphered.
Time's wheel frets on his finger still,
He bends no more his weight with time's;
He wept, as loud as wind,
And sleeps, with an indifferent will.
Not airs, not climes unclose behind
The lashes' never-faltering jet
Which star is his since Hesper set.

The Reminder

All night there had sought in vain
To coax a sullen eye,
(And pressed to the black pane
The brilliance of their sky)
The winter moon blown high,
And the starred and the clouded train.

They have passed me glittering,
And I heard tone on tone
Of the cold nightchime ring,
With will that churned alone
And sight pinned bleak as stone
To what the heart could bring.

Till now the night wears thin,
A roof leans out awry,
And cocks and wheels begin;
And from past morning-cry
A lone, a steadfast eye
Silently looks in.

Bell which Chides to Peace

Bell, bell which chides to peace
A moment of a falling street,
Repeat the hour, repeat
From the many winding feet
Light ebbs without cease.
Bell which speaks the instant rest,
An image of remembered time
Dispels the gathered instant from the breast.
Clock struck, and sky's achime,
Bell strikes, and I saw rise
Images whereon now
Surrendered passion lies:
Saw, as death might start from sleep
To gaze upon the living brow.
Then what watch shall passion keep,
Deep as all their hollow eyes?
Passion never watched so well,
Lost is their gaze as deep,
Bell says, and bell.

Kingdom of Heaven

Bleak the February light
On the dark threshold spread;
The frost stood thick against the lock,
The clock for the great cold stopped dead,
When old wits idle as their luck
Woke singing in the bed,
That heard while white frost span by night
A pigeon happy with its bread.

And sang: "I wakened to a sound
That the streams make at thaw;
And pity on the shape I found
Inside a looking-glass with light.
For looking on my heart I saw
A time before the break of day,
And looking won to second sight,
And cast my character away.

"The fields lie bound beneath the sky,
The hedgetop and the furrow freeze;
And still old ploughwheels sigh,
As sweet as bones which stretch from sleep;
And sooner than their sound is by
Will come a noise of yellow bees
When the hay is nodding deep,
And some wise throat which laughs for ease."

Till there was a soft voice that spoke:
"Hush, for all the sound you tell

Is out of an old horn I blew.
I am come down to see who woke
On earth's cold brink when night was through.
No wilder chance befell
Than the starry breath I drew:
I am Gabriel."

Alas, Kind Element!

Then I was sealed, and like the wintering tree
I stood me locked upon a summer core;
Living, had died a death, and asked no more.
And I lived then, but as enduringly,
And my heart beat, but only as to be.
Ill weathers well, hail, gust and cold I bore,
I held my life as hid, at root, in store:
Thus I lived then, till this air breathed on me.
Till this kind air breathed kindness everywhere,
There where my times had left me I would stay.
Then I was staunch, I knew nor yes nor no;
But now the wishful leaves have thronged the air.
My every leaf leans forth upon the day;
Alas, kind element! which comes to go.

The Walk

A walk above the waters' side,
None else to hearken there was come,
Where through haunt green and wellaway
I watched the low brook waters glide.
The heart rose stifling where it lay:
A voice dwelt there and was dumb.

The waters glided wellaway,
Hoarfast-hasting, jewel-swung;
And still that sound went breathing by
Of what they all at last would say;
An ear could overcatch the cry,
Though yet not all its tone was wrung.

The will shall learn itself alone,
For walking by the waters' side,
At every step my ear I bowed,
And heard from rift and runnelstone:
Away, they told delight aloud,
Away, it was the heart replied.

Recollection of the Wood

Light at each point was beating then to flight,
The sapling bark flushed upward, and the welling
Tips of the wood touched, touched at the bound,
And boughs were slight and burdened beyond telling
Toward that caress of the boughs a summer's night,
Illimitable in fragrance and in sound.

Here were the blue buds, earlier than hope,
Unnumbered, beneath the leaves, a breath apart,
Wakening in root-dusk. When the air went north,
Lifting the oakleaves from the northern slope,
Their infinite young tender eyes looked forth.
Here all that was, was frail to bear a heart.

This Severing

I turned as new resigned:
A summer gleaned, my business was within,
My charge the sober mind,
My care the wintry bin.

And found the boughs in stain,
Past-promise-hued. O not
Before, earnest as rich was yet so plain;
A harvest was ungot.

Beech drenching down my pathway goldenheart,
Ash, pensive light-cheek rose,
Both pluck the thought apart,
And meant you, heart, to close?

So fell the doomed farewells;
So, so looked forth a thing:
Regret, reproach, what else
Must baffle, vex, beguile this severing.

The Apple in Its Season

It will be this: the apple in its season,
With what withheld, what given,
All fallen under heaven,
At last is reason.

So still the year's revivals have their air
Of passion for the part;
Loyally even the heart
Wrings pride, act, despair;

Until the ceremony of old sight
Can yield a leaf, a leaf
That more than wish or grief
Which its true lover might;

And boughs bringing the apple in its season,
The crooktrunk at the road
Stooped with its crazier load,
Become the reason.

This Measure

This measure was a measure to my mind,
Still musical through the unlikely hush.
The cold goes wide as doors, and in will come
Those notes of May set ringing through the brush,
Where every voice by natural law is dumb.

How many seasons I had watched the boughs,
That first are happy-tongued, and happy-leaved,
Then bleed as though an autumn were the last,
While that great life was with them undeceived,
Which all a wintering world seals home more fast.

Now visibly indeed I am assailed,
And yet indeed have safe a veriest thing,
And now I learn I only asked as much.
It was in blooming weeks I lacked a spring
Rooted and blowing beyond sense or touch.

The Wood

Through the wind-bellying wood
Cruder spite than the wind
Has rent the leaves of the mind,
And whipped the gale to winnow,
For pulse and sap are blind;
Has ringed its worm to devour
All the laborious branch
Laboured of memory;
So blast and rot have the hour,
And sinew and air scream,
Because too lofty a thing
Withers in mastery;
Too long a pride upflings,
To fling that diagram
Against the harrowing sky.

The Runner with the Lots

We listen, wind from where,
And two have heard
The step across the field
That went from us unseen,
The word that scarcely stirred
Along the corn's stiff green,
Or in their hair who bend among the corn.

And two have understood:
Though the great sails untorn
Of high September bear,
Toward harbour, earth and yield,
The amber-dwindled mood
Is come; the bronze, the blue,
And every hue entering a solitude.

And all about we seize,
Of all that summers knew
Or autumns reconciled,
Sense of some utmost thing,
Some clasp unransoming,
Proffered the destinies;
And on her face the look of its grave love.

Piercing on each, one air
Has touched them, earth and child;
And fairest here,
Fair now, whom love has sealed;
But fair unseen there move

Before us, unbeguiled,
The equal feet of love,
And the blind hands bearing the luck of the year.

Light at Equinox

A realm is here of masquing light
When struck rent wood and cornland by
The belled heaven claps the ground.
Husk, seed, pale straw, pale ear the year reposes,
And a thinned frieze of earth rims round
The whey-gleamed wet-ash-dimming sky,
And whole trodden floor of light,
Where that slant limb winds with its shadowing closes.

Distant as lustrally the sun,
Within that pearl of nimble play
Where traverse with rehearsing tread
Orients of prime to their all-reaping west,
Strangered from every grave glissade
Of blue enduskings or of milky day,
And wan, his silver nimbus on,
Muses his burning sojourn unprofessed.

Past barks mouse-sleek, wattled as serpent skin,
Rare acorn fall, rare squirrel flash.
Beyond, and in a silenced scene,
The wren, gamin wanderer of immense day
Can with luxuriant bendings preen,
Or in his pebble-scoopings plash,
To alarmless Eden flown,
And suddenly, for nothing, flies away.

And all are sole in the estranging day;
Forms of all things their candour wear,
Like the undefending dead,
And forth from out that mortal stricture gaze,
Of unperspective radiance shed
Through everywhere horizoned air,
Tasking precising love to say,
For its dense words, the azuring periphrase.

To her own brink light glides, intent
An unsphering sense to bind
By narrowing measures in.
Sidelong as then up branching March she bade
Stiff buds into the glancing skein,
And the green reel unwind;
Now toward another pole she's leant,
And netherwards for partner draws her shade.

The Summer Image

(From a Persian Carpet)

Ash and strewments, the first moth-wings, pale
Ardour of brief evenings, on the fecund wind;
Or all a wing, less than wind,
Breath of low herbs upfloats, petal or wing,
Haunting the musk precincts of burial.
For the season of newer riches moves triumphing,
Of the evanescence of deaths. These potpourris
Earth-tinctured, jet insect-bead, cinder of bloom—
How weigh while a great summer knows increase,
Ceaselessly risen, what there entombs:
Of candour fallen from the slight stems of Mays,
Corrupt of the rim a blue shades, pensively:
So a fatigue of wishes will young eyes.
And brightened, unpurged eyes of revery, now
Not to glance to fabulous groves again;
For now deep presence is, and binds its close,
And closes down the wreathed alleys escape of sighs.
And now rich time is weaving, hidden tree,
The fable of orient threads from bough to bough.
Old rinded wood, whose lissomeness within
Has reached from nothing to its covering
These many corymbs' flourish! —And the green
Shells which wait amber, breathing, wrought
Towards the still trance of summer's centering,
Motives by ravished humble fingers set,
Each in a noon of its own infinite.
And here is leant the branch and its repose

Of the deep leaf to the pilgrim plume. Repose,
Inflections brilliant and mute of the voyager, light!
And here the nests, and freshet throats resume
Notes over and over found, names
For the silvery ascensions of joy. Nothing is here
But moss and its bells now of the root's night;
But the beetle's bower, and arc from grass to grass
For the flight in gauze. Now its fresh lair,
Grass-deep, nestles the cool eft to stir
Vague newborn limbs, and the bud's dark winding has
Access of day. Now on the subtle noon
Time's image, at pause with being, labours free
Of all its charge, for each in coverts laid,
Of clement kind; and everlastingly,
In some elision of bright moments is known,
Changed wide as Eden, the branch whose silence sways
Dazzle of the murmurous leaves to continual tone;
Its separations, sighing to own again
Being of the ignorant wish; and sways to sight,
Waked from it nighted, the marvelous foundlings of light;
Risen and weaving from the ceaseless root
A divine ease whispers toward fruitfulness,
While all a summer's conscience tempts the fruit.

O Grave

How of our midst now, nearly, death beshades
A face that first upon the sole selves shone,
Their face for nearness; and its mimes too fade,
Which comforted remorse with chiding, gone,
Flickering foregoings, till new nothing is,
Dead-centered of our sense, the denser substance. More,
More than love was guilty for, that sees
It will not give her back, now, to herself,
Subdues the lucid featurer
In dark of things whose light is not their own.

Bird in its plumage and another, we are brought
To learn of others as we not wholly shall
Of selves. So niggling the corroder sought,
Where our stony foundings are corrupt to fill
The leech-mouths of the generated; tries,
As love for its bared element, still
In us all-isolate complicity;
Cool lord of chances, weighs among reductions
Eyes equal to the watch, and eyes
To pierce some maggotwork of history;

So ravels us his backwards sequences,
To unstitch the nursing vision, till life gone
Seem gone like a possession from the stilled thing,
Where in the flesh the flowery kingdom fails
The resurrection and the life of cells.
Or blank to compassion offers, quieting,
Never so known, beheld ineffably,

An eye that roves, unmaking maker, upon
Its look, first that had brided joy,
Shuffled and soiled among time's cuckoldries.

Thus moved to motion, mocked to stillness, thus
Leadenly jettisoned of days, for whom
A tribute of petals shone like derision from
Their kingdoms of perpetual innocency,
Unsuffered sacrifice, this being's goods
Is what it is, it is necessitous.
There are shrewd bargains on us to the crumb,
Even as shapes of matter, marvelously
A secret to itself and given beyond
Itself, the fallen attitudes
Which the silt and the trodden lives are avenged upon.

And choice, grown act, where past our ignorance
And her wish, outnumbering chance makes clear,
Makes wise in its obtuse inheritance:
Into our wilderness the grain is spent,
Shattering the unwilling husks. Beginning to hear
What is asked, ask wonder for its sight,
Our logic's and our love's admonishment,
That of this midst there was of her poised shining,
What had owed nothing, like the grave,
But she was given for from her own night;

Ungrudging from this darkness and this ground,
Discernlessly the reaping and the sown;
As often from our midst, blest most herself,

The more itself in that it in itself
Approved, approving its delight. *For this*
Was not a way, but darkness and a ground.
Yet had she been an all unchosenness,
Only in this rejoicing was her own,
As a secret kept, fragrant forever,
And across all their thresholds lost and found.

What do we figuring that obedient heart
In the certain gravity of its motion? —Light,
Intolerably, a motion of the heart,
If the burden were itself the lightness. As
Often then or death or we beshaded,
Slanting dark outward unconfounded, some sight
Was thus and deathful, then of our midst how nearly;
Some sight in us veered ever here and deathwards,
Never enough, enough persuaded
Of all her fragrant secrecy spoke clearly.

Goodbye Those Children

Goodbye, those children had learned to say, Last looks!
At the cove, at from under the pines, at the rock and the
　　dunes!
But no leavetaking was ceremony for the once-seen,
What the Undines left, and the unimagined ones
Of their mornings all air and sea before children were,
And the children used to put some in a box.
And then they were driven away, and the green
Willowfalls came pouring, leaves wove deep
On deeper, till at her lacepapered stand
They saw, through asters' waning blue, like sleep—
Fringed children's eyes, some girl with a faint neck
Drooped as dwarves' daisies and the one-stemmed blooms
　　you find
Where the forests are mown back; with tendril hair
Fine as the grasses that stand up in moss;
And when they had bought her honey and jam, a hand
And hand would wave, a child would peep behind,
Not waving then, only half grudging that
Alone still in summer's fringes she sat,
To be left warden of all summer thus,
O through an unimagined winter there,
Or to bide with another child through another sleep.

For on past the tall hedgerows waving high
Their red riches was that other cave,
Its world, as in a wave, to look within,
Smaller and smaller, and let its flickered shade
Wind with you somewhere, and on its paths you'd made
To help ants to their hill, a spider drag

Its white belly-bag along; and lay
Your arms about, an earth with creatures in,
And think it all would never come to harm.
Needs must be sorrowful then to have gone away,
Not even knowing it, with no goodbye,
Farewelling ways, for what one nearly is.
And the lilacs held their earlier cave, kept whole
And tidy of itself, with the blue egg
Bits mosaiced, but the birds dropped lime,
And a snail left its partly wilted shell.

Then was remembered what there were pains to save,
And the stones were their different colors, but the caress
Had waned, as it will wane, of all sea-brightness,
And dry, dry, powdered and rubbed away,
The rosied nacre with its dews of mauve.
And in the box, amongst its eery smell,
Mortal and stiff the starry arms were rayed,
That reached reminding from some other time
And this, how fallen a thing can lie, still much
As first, odd fossil flower or monster, still
Singular, crusted with itself, as when
Its thorns curled shrinking from the wondering touch.

Now solitude in summer receives
What none may act on, from suave throats,
Anxiousness which depraves;
And failed the concert of the notes
Left by the deaf musician, dead
Unpraised, a cavern of bone they tread
Through to triumphs of air, I watch glow,
Unearthly green, whose wincings call
At the pane, and of vibrancies
Unprobed about a radio,
A lamp, a heart for plucking, seize
A tempo exquisitely small.

And ballet of sentience, I draw near:
This balance on six green nerves, from night
By our crude light entangled, supposes
Walks taken almost upon
Presentiment. The wings' sheath sere,
Freshness immense, a body shown
Whose twinkling chemistry transposes
Earth's first, essential supper to flight.
And I know you, sad straggler, one
Of a numberless people. The feast of the tree
Is forward, your tents I hear
Resound with long voracity.

What weak small members to prepare
For assumption to the natural!
Touch of the pathos exhaled here,
And human beneficence will fall

Back from contraction it must bear
At an inexorable frontier.
And as pure horror. You too appal.
Lives now not often practise near,
With the awe's name, it may be, lost
Awe of a severance earlier known
Fissured within, once somehow crossed,
Not of ourselves, and not alone.

And you, poor host, whose shrilling cries
Believe you slip time's scrutiny
In ceaseless summer to pillage, concern
Of larger empery than his,
In stratagem not we discern,
Again upon doomed forays launches,
And seems not tender of your chances:
Those trim accoutrements they dispense
By their frail colour carelessly
Expose you where August advances
Through the burdened and sombering branches
Of a season turned somnolence.

The Font in the Forest

Before remembrance we moved here, withheld,
This long reserve beneath what has not been,
Without commencement, late by life that lay,
Offered for anyone and still its own;
Intrusion of its utter forest whose eyes
Abash (nested and laired how deep) which dwell
In their intent. Here on the foreheads dries
The christening freshness of the clear year's front.
And all comes docile to its names, and all
The specious air of creature cannot shield
Unenterable recess. O listener!
Who had not heard the name you listened for,
Beside a font, tongueless, which lichens tinge
With chill frescoings, where of day
On day sad afterlight must fall
Changeless upon the falling of a day
Lichens in frond with their dim arms adore.

The People in the Park

Under the mock-oranges the children spy,
Where the sod leaves the mould-greened ground,
Underneath the sweet shrub and the mass of June,
Shaping of them soft posture and bird-cry,
Reaving the aimless glances, and have not found
The cause of seeking, or whether the pure cocoon
Of the silk and sheen of being is given to rend.

Liker, and all less like than leaves the eyes,
Unmet, in whose glance the trembled irises
Ward the still anthers of will's secrecy,
As out of the child's vision his ancient wishes pass,
Risen from the devoured garden flesh, and come
In the freshness of flowers, into the daylight womb,
His limbs that bear them with offended grace.

And one is offered elsewhere for his own,
Annunciations, whisperings, to be
More intimately strangered to the bone.
And in the hearts whose many a hope were seen
Stranger than its befallen, than seed more hid,
The plumule's hieroglyph and more hid than these
By petalling days, beneath what has not been,

And in the bodies drying like dried wood,
Nighted, a center and a solitude,
Is an abiding. O not for a life young
Alone seek the old looking hearts that have

Green, green to gaze upon forever this scene,
And look as with the longing of the grave,
As on the times they were consumed among.

Then shall it not have been life young alone
Darkness dimensioned, in all things' cradle lain,
But in the hearts of cooling ash intent
Is its abiding, beneath what has not been,
When all has been foretelling to be spent,
As from its sacred cause of presence then,
Where it is nothing, one with its assent.

Gold shed upon suckling gold,
The time of the bole blackens,
Of the dark mounted through dapple,
While in the sealed apple
The seed cradled toward cold.
A gold on gold spent,
Put by from an elm in its years
Now its gilded of days,
Over turf's dishevelment;
Where all which is green sickens,
All the fresh shall be sere.
All which is green sickens,
And it is but for a time
Those embered veinings blaze
A year's delirium;
Or neared of other space,
Unportioned azure shall close
One of more, and which is,
One which goes.
Let the little pupils that will,
Of vision, gaze for salt
To whet their gazing, wit
In one weather is high
From burrow and lair, by
Nether providences' default
An all's accrued.
And apposite, beyond
Such primer beholdings, has
Its long accounting known

The beetle's morsel thus
Was rich, and the slug's bed on
The oak's generations, deep
Over the lark's bones.
In slough of Edens fast
Wit in one weather shall stand,
While millennia nibble at
The sensual apple
Toppled it net,
Plenty in the palm of the hand,
And the fallen not fallen, not lost
From out its certitude—
For our unbeggaring
Has been gross. Few and late
To cherish an immoderate
Wish, hope's calculus,
Love's hope; few to miss,
From natural tally thrust,
In the lime-girdled space
Of choice, where alone
Man can abandon what
Is only his own;
And in cold and tarrying
Their rearisers sleep:

While to the granite cheek
Light's purples bring
Infinite their ministering,
And past our finial
And ragged crests, to keep

Time's ambient stood,
Propose horizons from
Their shadowy quarries; while,
In an unwandered wood,
Or under the indifferent foot,
Is let fall, let fall a fruit,
Through eternal leisures down,
For but time's unravelling.

Thoughts on a Violet

Not now in the florist's window seen: within,
Reminding memory, smelt through glass.
For here the violet was
Still in the offering hand
That quarrelled after; then,
Early, a fragrance strayed
Withering from the dead's muff; and led
In traverse of mind's subterfuge perfecter
And far, borne memoried beyond
The seasons told,
Shone, vegetative star,
Risen and passing, after the summers told,
The winters' patience, lent,
Exchange of darkness, where the tread
Of yearning, still visitant,
Arched not to bruise an emblematic head.

As if! As if! Yet there, yet known through glass,
Any of all
The stiff-stuck rounds, not one
In hypostasis, a violet *was*.
It had the fierce propriety to be,
And its distinction bear,
If indiscernible where, dazzlingly,—
Rankness or hue, the deep-fresh which
Alone the looking at may touch—
If indiscernible it were,
Where imperturbably a violet bore,
Perished to perishing version gone,
Such stamp, in all memberings commingled still,

That bore, with all our rushed contingency,
And bore, in every shred, unmatchable
And hid, the imprint of the manying one.

Unplucked from its clutch of context! Surcharge of all
My years, uncertain, beckoned for,
Sooner went dizzying from their literal
And trod on of perceiving; fared
Our divagations, a life's anguish come,
Sigher and solipsist, the way prepared,
Into a sadness of Elysium;—
To trip with these, pressed through an eternal chink,
Nosegay of nothing's bosom! Yet that might
Embedded lie, where poise from the abyss,
There always rose this brink
Of our enactment. Time has no site
To pitch such purples on, as thought with this
For one vein's one thread would think, and thus to think,
Thought's cell, heart's soddener
One part us there for vesture, mind and care.

Homesick for the unlived, before its bloom I stood,
Till the just props surprised those charlatans
Of being the scene directs beyond mischance.
Importuned body and bone,
Whose many wisdoming shades have asked it blood
For speech; criss-cross
With desire, wrench of thus
Palpable only its force, late must
The life learn, late, that improvised from within,

Its own materiality all calls,
Some tears' withdrawals amid.—
Pure tear which guilt deflects, and judgment stains,
Whose sorrower the nonce all prompts that will
Ask matter for love, act from dust; still, still
Verging abysms upon
Still a recalcitrance.

POEMS: *A Selection*

II: *As Apt Was Joy*

As apt was joy
And subtle cap-a-pie
In time to mortice me,
Loyal and dure accord,
Now all my times exacts me.

Bell Tower

I have seen, desolate one, the voice has its tower;
The voice also, builded at secret cost,
Its temple of precious tissue. Not silent then
Forever—casting silence in your hour.

There marble boys are leant from the light throat,
Thick locks that hang with dew and eyes dewlashed,
Dazzled with morning, angels of the wind,
With ear a-point for the enchanted note.

And these at length shall tip the hanging bell,
And first the sound must gather in deep bronze,
Till, clearer than ice, purer than a bubble of gold,
It beat in the sky and the air and the ear's remorseless well.

Country Summer

Now the rich cherry, whose sleek wood,
And top with silver petals traced
Like a strict box its gems encased,
Has spilt from out that cunning lid,
All in an innocent green round,
Those melting rubies which it hid;
With moss ripe-strawberry-encrusted,
So birds get half, and minds lapse merry
To taste that deep-red, lark's-bite berry,
And blackcap bloom is yellow-dusted.

The wren that thieved it in the eaves
A trailer of the rose could catch
To her poor droopy sloven thatch,
And side by side with the wren's brood—
O lovely time of beggar's luck—
Opens the quaint and hairy bud;
And full and golden is the yield
Of cows that never have to house,
But all night nibble under boughs,
Or cool their sides in the moist field.

Into the rooms flow meadow airs,
The warm farm baking smell's blown round.
Inside and out, and sky and ground
Are much the same; the wishing star,
Hesperus, kind and early born,
Is risen only finger-far;
All stars stand close in summer air,

And tremble, and look mild as amber;
When wicks are lighted in the chamber,
They are like stars which settled there.

Now straightening from the flowery hay,
Down the still light the mowers look,
Or turn, because their dreaming shook,
And they waked half to other days,
When left alone in the yellow stubble
The rusty-coated mare would graze.
Yet thick the lazy dreams are born,
Another thought can come to mind,
But like the shivering of the wind,
Morning and evening in the corn.

The River in the Meadows

Crystal parting the meads,
A boat drifted up it like a swan.
Tranquil, dipping his bright front to the waters,
A slow swan is gone.

Full waters, O flowing silver,
Clear, level with the clover,
They will stain drowning a star,
With the moon they will brim over.

Running through lands dewy and shorn,
Cattle stoop at its brink,
And every tawny-colored throat
Will sway its bells and drink.

I saw a boat sailing the meadows
With a tranced gait. It seemed
Loosed by a spell from its moorings,
Or a thing the helmsman dreamed.

And I thought it could carry no traveller,
For the vessel would go down,
If a heart were heavy-winged,
Or the bosom it dwelt in stone.

Acquittal

The barbarous bird,
It will not tame.
The plumage glistening over straw,
O the wild thing snared,
Will set me at shame.

It was decoyed,
But cannot change.
Its wing with beating lonely air,
Its beak with tasting wilderness berry,
Its look and lovely flight are strange.

What lover sullen,
What love all paltering,
Possesses the gold bough of heaven,
Or who loving
Beset the royal wandering thing?

Dearest, beauty, begone.
The eye holds you, dreaming apart;
Go, dearest and beauty,
Pursued but by the heart, driven longing
After the savage heart.

The Moon and Spectator

In the dead of the night
I got from my bed;
The air stretched hollow,
A theatre of the dead.

The night was half sunk and the wind gone,
The passion of the wind had gone down;
But the boughs shaken a little, blanched a little,
Spectrally, by the moon.

The moon performed her march fantastic,
The harrier of clouds, a flame half seen,
Or full in the high sky, the royal sables being spread,
A withered queen.

The moon, that chill frame, I saw enact
Her rite commemorative of a bound ghost,
And thought of a night wildly born, outliving storm,
And its tears lost.

Almost without pulse, a spectator to the moon,
A dream of some fashion set the body awake,
But called to the heart in the deeps of sleep how rising
From sleep again it would break.

A fall over rock,
Metal answering to water,
Is the seal of this spot;
A land trodden by music
And the tune forgot.

Of a region savage,
The territory that was broken,
Silver gushed free;
And earth holy, earth meek shall receive it
In humility.

This, not dwelt in, this haunted,
The country of the proud,
Is curdling to stone,
And careless of the feet of the waters
As they glance from it down.

Sundown

This is the time lean woods shall spend
A steeped-up twilight, and the pale evening drink,
And the perilous roe, the leaper to the west brink,
Trembling and bright to the caverned cloud descend.

Now shall you see pent oak gone gusty and frantic,
Stooped with dry weeping, ruinously unloosing
The sparse disheveled leaf, or reared and tossing
A dreary scarecrow bough in funeral antic.

Then, tatter you and rend,
Oak heart, to your profession mourning; not obscure
The outcome, not crepuscular; on the deep floor
Sable and gold match lustres and contend.

And rags of shrouding will not muffle the slain.
This is the immortal extinction, the priceless wound
Not to be staunched. The live gold leaks beyond,
And matter's sanctified, dipped in a gold stain.

The Horn

While hastening to the feast I found
A venerable silver-throated horn,
Which were I brave enough to sound,
Then all, as from that moment born,
Would breathe the honey of this clime,
And three times merry in their time,
Would praise the virtue of the horn.

The mist is risen like thin breath,
The young leaves of the ground smell chill,
And faintly are they strewn on death
The road I came down a west hill;
But quickening with its name I name
The slender creature-brightening flame
Since bones have caught their marrow chill.

And in a thicket passed me by,
In the black brush, a running hare,
Having a spectre in his eye,
That sped in darkness to the snare;
And ever since I know in pride,
The heart, set beating in the side,
Has but the wisdom of a hare.

Evening Sky

How now are we tossed about by a windy heaven,
The eye that scans it madded to discern
In a single quarter all the wild ravage of light;
Amazing light to quiver and suddenly turn
Before the stormy demon fall of night,
And yet west spaces saved celestial
With silver sprinklings of the anointed sun.
The eye goes up for certitude,
Driven hither and thither on that shifty scene
To the dome closing like impenetrable hoar,
And down from the cold zenith drops abashed;
O desolation rent by intolerable blue
Of the living heaven's core,
Nor death itself at last the heavenly whim.
For how can an eye sustain
To watch heaven slain and quickening, or do
To stretch in its little orbit and contain
Sky balancing chaos in an inconstant rim?

Lullaby

Hush, lullay.
Your treasures all
Encrust with rust,
Your trinket pleasures fall
    To dust.
Beneath the sapphire arch,
Upon the grassy floor,
Is nothing more
    To hold,
And play is over-old.
Your eyes
    In sleepy fever gleam,
Their lids droop
    To their dream.
You wander late alone,
The flesh frets on the bone,
Your love fails in your breast;
Here is the pillow.
    Rest.

Twilit Revelation

This hour was set the time for heaven's descent,
Come drooping toward us on the heavy air,
The sky, that's heaven's seat, above us bent,
Blue faint as violet ash, you near me there
In nether space, so drenched in goblin blue
I could touch Hesperus as soon as you.

Now I perceive you, lapped in singling light,
Washed by that blue which sucks whole planets in,
And hung like those top jewels of the night
A mournful gold too high for love to win.
And you, poor brief, poor melting star, you seem
Half to sink, half to brighten in that stream.

And these rich-bodied hours of our delight
Show like a mothwing's substance when the fall
Of confine-loosing, blue, unending night
Extracts the spirit of this temporal.
So space can pierce the crevice wide between
Fast hearts, skies deep-descended intervene.

More than the lovely who prevail?
But very love must know
By no perduring thing
Can this be known.
Though with attributes of marble,
It is a mortal beauty
Never hewn in stone.

To what they loved and destroyed,
Never had their fill of cherishing and would not save,
Even the gods fixed no star;
But more in sign
The rainbow's meltings and the reed
And the slight narcissus gave.

Counsel to Unreason

These lovers' inklings which our loves enmesh,
Lost to the cunning and dimensional eye,
Though tenemented in the selves we see,
Not more perforce than azure to the sky,
Were necromancy-juggled to the flesh,
And startled from no daylight you or me.

For trance and silverness those moons commend,
Which blanch the warm life silver-pale; or look
What ghostly portent mist distorts from slight
Clay shapes; the willows that the waters took
Liquid and brightened in the waters bend,
And we, in love's reflex, seemed loved of right.

Then no more think to net forthwith love's thing,
But cast for it by spirit sleight-of-hand;
Then only in the slant glass contemplate,
Where lineament outstripping line is scanned,
Then on the perplexed text leave pondering,
Love's proverb is set down transliterate.

The Mysterious Thing

What plummet, seas, to sound you—
All the long reaches spun out silver-white,
Turn you and cast drowned riches?
Or how again, O velvet night,
When the sky, stooping with its glittering load,
About the elf-locks of the curious grass
Scatters its sparklings, will you part almost
Upon the quintessential host?

Or how the figment spirit, sleeping,
Can it render body, ghost,
In its dream unseat the heavy monarch,
Conjure to the bleak wild coast
Its sunk, its deep delight,
Its night and mist divide, recall how flitting
Above the pallid thing,
Joy has an azure wing?

Every Bird of Nature

Every bird of nature
Has a true wing,
Save one that has the feather
Of a foreign thing.
The pulse in his bosom was so luckless and wild
He spied a feather in the grass
And plucked it from the bright dews lying,
Brighter than dew with witcheries . . .
So ever false he flies.

The thicket of birds
Is quivering with wings,
And freshly there when bush is in sprig,
The linnet sings.
But the bird that I name,
Though with a gentle body,
Must nest him in a flame,
And calls to his love,
The bird that I tell,
A Love fare you well.

You should have fashioned
Your musician, Death,
Of the strung wires,
Cold air his breath.
Dearest and last you bound
In a dark harmony;
It has a sweet sound;
But death's a cruel note,
Set in a mortal throat.

The Lament of Quarry

The hunter of huntsmen bred
That looked on his quarry slain
The lament of quarry made:
"Would you had your quickness again!
Gracious and light, apart,
Stepping on velvet feet;
It is heavy on my heart.

"A true, a fast decoy all night in sleep
I set lest any rove,
Snares I planted, subtle and deep;
It was no guile, but love.
The gentle entered without fright
And bent upon the hunter's look
Their eyes of delicate light.

"Of my father's father I got a proud steed,
And a barb of my father I took—
O cunning barb by which you bleed—
But a white hind gave me suck.
For I was cradled in hardihood,
But a mild doe, but the hind pity,
With strangeness thinned my blood.

"Fierce and beauteous the hawk,
Then where is the natureless creature
That has confusion for kind?
To the greyhound his fleet foot,
To the moorlark her light wing,
And the waste track of being to the mind."

The Lonely Host

Cast on the turning wastes of wind
Are cords that none can touch or see,
Are threads of subtle ore which bind
The grains of wandering air to peace.
If any stretch a hand to find
How fast, how gold a stuff it be,
He will but dizzy the poor mind
With bending from the steeps of peace;
And though rest catch him in once more,
He is bewildered there, like birds
The storm beat to the door.

The day comes wildly up the east,
Because the cup of vision broke,
And those clear silver floods released
Go ravaging the calm sky of night;
And all who to that seeing woke
Look coldly on a common sight,
As to outstare substantial stuff.
The substance never is enough
When lids are drenched apart by light.
Before the light shall fade again
They drag a shadow forth from it
To print upon the barren brain.

And though when lips are parched to tell
What brooded on the lips too long,
They quench them at a noisy well,
The noise of waters is so sweet
They say, The heart has ease of this,

And no more all its burden is
Than the catch of an old song;
And then to a lost catch repeat
The carking woe, the little bliss:
Like things every mortal hears,
But these tell them in a tongue
Barbarous to your ears.

Ghostly Tree

O beech, unbind your yellow leaf, for deep
The honeyed time lies sleeping, and lead shade
Seals up the eyelids of its golden sleep.
Long are your flutes, chimes, your small bells at rest,
And here is only the cold scream of the fox,
Only the huntsman following on the hound;
While your quaint-plumaged,
The bird that your green summer boughs lapped round,
Bends south its soft bright breast.

Before the winter and the terror break,
Scatter the leaf that broadened with the rose
Not for a tempest, but a sigh, to take.
Four nights to exorcise the thing that stood
Bound by these frail which dangle at your branch,
They ran a frosty dagger to its heart;
And that wan substance
No more remembered it might cry or start
Or stain a point with blood.

The Rounds and Garlands Done

Now the golden looks are spent
And light no more will brim from the large air,
But green and changeling drips from the little round
Of the close branch;
While the shadow, born of nothing,
Glides over the green ground.

Day that cast the lovely looks is sped,
And from the turf, circled with white dew,
The lovers and the children are gone;
Leaving the wreath, the bouquet fresh, looped up with
   grasses.
All the golden looks are spent,
And the time of the rounds and the garlands done.

High from a drowning heart the waters' cry
Rises subdued to silver and is lost
On the pure bell of silence, where the petal
Whose sweetness drooped the spray,
Drained now of lustre, rides
Upon a soundless wind
More light than any ghost.

So wide the wells of darkness sink,
These, having their own light, that are lost with the light,
Appear, immersed in mournfulness over the night,
Like things that in sleep will come to the mind's brink:
The bright Aldebaran and seven that hover,
Seven wild and pale, clouding their brightness over;
And the flame that fell with summer, and the rose of stars
    returning,
Like tears piercing the sky,
Glittering without cause, for the piece of a legend,
Wept I know not why,
As none can say,
As countless they weep
Ranging without fold beyond the order of day—
The brightmost, the forgotten,
Gathered only of sleep,
All night upon the lids set burning,
Shaken from the lids of morning.

Sleep to Waking

The mind that a dream left sullen
Turns to the cold clouded light
And broods as on a thing lifted from sleep,
Upon the bough that shows its bodily leaves
Colored like shadows, withdrawing them from night;
Pondering how many nights ago,
Nested among those leaves, the marvelous flock
Was telling with its many honey tongues
The tale of sleep; or if those leaves or no,
Since now an elder mind must climb so deep
Into sleep's well, after such image there,
Or stranger nature, if it come at all,
It will come unremembering out of sleep.

To Unconscionable Sound

Go, fill the bell of the wind
With the sweet unconscionable sound;
Do not breathe on the mind:
It is an indifferent shell,
Long whittled underwave,
And had no timbre's form
When the glittering wave withdrew
But what its waters gave.
Go twist the wind to a bell,
Or let it whip and turn
To any change you will
The visionary cloud;
They are innocent essence still.
But not the brooding heart,
A cloud that wraps about
The tempest it outwept,
And elemented then,
When the cold fancy rose
Which shakes off a heart like a dream
In the hollow where it slept.

For Harvest

The year turns to its rest.
Up from the earth, the fields, the early-fallen dew,
Moves the large star at evening, Arcturus low with autumn,
And summer calls in her many voices upon the frost.

I who have not seen for weeping
The plum ripen and fall, or the yellowing sheaf,
Am not unmindful now of the season that came and went,
The hours that told off freshness,
The bud and the rich leaf.

Though I turned aside before the summer
And weathered but a season of the mind,
Let me sit among you when the husk is stripped,
Let me tell by the bright grain,
Those labours in an acre of cloud and the reap of the wind.

Windy Way

The wind comes fast at heels with time
And bends the yellow tops of hay,
And somewhere on the running wind
I cast a thing I had away.
It was my life, or so I said,
And I did well, forsaking it,
To go as quickly as the dead.
For more than every traveller wise,
They're off before their dawdling kin
Can drop the pennies on their eyes;
Knowing it would be vain to tell,
Who have so vast a leave in mind,
If all night long a fare you well.

I did not give a backward look,
Yet could remember, if I would,
The lost was twenty jewels' worth
And nearer to my heart than blood;
And "Leave me here," its mourner cried,
And in God's truth I think I did,
Because I have so free a side;
And past the hollow ribs a bird
By chance came in, and ever since,
And light as grass, his voice is heard,
Telling how those true wings are met,
Which tumbled from the lying skein
And the grave tangle of the net.

Caryatid

Not at midnight, not at morning, O sweet city,
Shall we come in at your portal, but this girl,
Bearing on her head a broken stone,
In the body shaped to this, the throat and bosom
Poised no less for the burden now the temple is fallen,
Tells the white Athenian wonder overthrown.

There is no clasp which stays beauty forever.
Time has undone her, from porphyry, from bronze.
She is winged every way and will not rest;
But the gesture of the lover shall remain long after,
Where lovely and imponderable there leans
A weight more grave than marble on the breast.

Early Waking

Four hooves rang out and now are still.
In the dark wall the casements hold
Essential day above each sill,
Just light, and colored like thin gold.
Behind those hooves a drowsy course
All night I rode where hearts were clear,
And wishes blessèd at the source,
And for no shape of time stop here.

No more to raise that lively ghost
Which ran quicksilver to the bone:
By a whim's turn the whole was lost
When all its marrow worth was known.
Ghosts can cast shadows in the breast,
And what was present tears to weep,
Not heart nor mind would bid from rest
As fast as sorrow's, ten years deep.

I travel, not for a ghost's sake,
One step from sleep, and not for one
Left sleeping at my side I wake.
Before bricks rosy with the dawn,
The hooves will sound beyond the light:
There are dark roads enough to go
To last us through the end of night,
And I will make my waking slow.

It was for unconcerning light
That has not fallen on earth, to stare
An instant only out of night
And with night's cloudy character,
Before the laden mind shall slip
Past dream and on to brightmost dream
And fetterless high morning dip
Her two cold sandals in the stream.

Song from a Country Fair

When tunes jigged nimbler than the blood
And quick and high the bows would prance
And every fiddle string would burst
To catch what's lost beyond the string,
While half afraid their children stood,
I saw the old come out to dance.
The heart is not so light at first,
But heavy like a bough in spring.

Valhalla for the Living

Today he sickens with his hurt,
And straight behind the ribs it drove,
Tipped with more bitter mystery
Than a fresh heart is master of;
But only once young hardihood
Can seem to cost the heart its blood.

For time will mix his blood with wit,
And easy will he rise and go
To have a dozen merry wars,
And never wincing for the foe.
So all the ghostly heroes play
Whose wounds are healed at close of day.

Song

Wind blows over the heart
But the heart is fast in the breast,
So only give a sigh after the wind.
A heart that is pinned to the wind
Turns in the side without rest.

Or if you will bear in mind
A stream and the swan gone,
Scattering from its cold plumage the drops of the foam,
Then liken the heart rather
To the stream sailed of a swan.

Kennst du das Land

No, I have borne in mind this hill,
For once before I came its way
In hours when summer held her breath
Above her innocents at play;
Knew the leaves deepening the green ground
With their green shadows, there as still
And perfect as leaves stand in air;
The bird who takes delight in sound
Giving his young and watery call,
That is each time as if a fall
Flashed silver and were no more there.
And knew at last, when day was through,
That sky in which the boughs were dipped
More thick with stars than fields with dew;
And in December brought to mind
The laughing child to whom they gave
Among these slopes, upon this grass,
The summer-hearted name of love.
Still can you follow with your eyes,
Where on the green and gilded ground
The dancers will not break the round,
The beechtrunks carved of moonlight rise;
Still at their roots the violets burn
Lamps whose flame is soft as breath.
But turn not so, again, again,
They clap me in their wintry chain;
I know the land whereto you turn,
And know it for a land of death.

Magnificat in Little

I was enriched, not casting after marvels,
But as one walking in a usual place,
Without desert but common eyes and ears,
No recourse but to hear, power but to see,
Got to love you of grace.

Subtle musicians, that could body wind,
Or contrive strings to anguish, in conceit
Random and artless strung a branch with bells,
Fixed in one silver whim, which at a touch
Shook and were sweet.

And you, you lovely and unpurchased note,
One run distraught, and vexing hot and cold
To give to the heart's poor confusion tongue,
By chance caught you, and henceforth all unlearned
Repeats you gold.

The Figurehead

This that is washed with weed and pebblestone
Curved once a dolphin's length before the prow,
And I who read the land to which we bore
In its grave eyes, question my idol now,
What cold and marvelous fancy it may keep,
Since the salt terror swept us from our course,
Or if a wisdom later than the storm,
For old green ocean's tinctured it so deep;
And with some reason to me on this strand
The waves, the ceremonial waves have come,
And stooped their barbaric heads, and all flung out
Their glittering arms before them, and are gone,
Leaving the murderous tribute lodged in sand.

Send Forth the High Falcon

Send forth the high falcon flying after the mind
Till it come toppling down from its cold cloud:
The beak of the falcon to pierce it till it fall
Where the simple heart is bowed.
O in wild innocence it rides
The rare ungovernable element,
But once it sways to terror and descent,
The marches of the wind are its abyss,
No wind staying it upward of the breast—
Let mind be proud for this,
And ignorant from what fabulous cause it dropt,
Or with how learned a gesture the unschooled heart
Shall lull both terror and innocence to rest.

Time and Spirit

Spirit going with me here,
If you tell the time aright,
It's by some ancestral clock
Older than the golden sun,
And his measure trod with night.

Rarely by my calendar
Bite or sup for you is spread,
Yet you come not grace forgone
As the jostling starvelings do,
But most mannerly are fed.

All my store consumes to keep
This poor lamp which kindles me.
You that take no thought to live
In an exquisite excess
Spend more brightness than I see.

How should you and I keep step?
Threescore ten was set my race
Of just distancing the worm;
And a lifetime to a sphere
Lends a more exalted pace.

The Mount

Now I have tempered haste,
The joyous traveller said,
The steed has passed me now
Whose hurrying hooves I fled.
My spectre rides thereon,
I learned what mount he has,
Upon what summers fed;
And wept to know again,
Beneath the saddle swung,
Treasure for whose great theft
This breast was wrung.
His bridle bells sang out,
I could not tell their chime,
So brilliantly he rings,
But called his name as Time.
His bin was morning light,
Those straws which gild his bed
Are of the fallen West.
Although green lands consume
Beneath their burning tread,
In everlasting bright
His hooves have rest.

Many Mansions

The last majority attained,
And shut from its small house of dust,
Into the heritage of air
The spirit goes because it must:
And halts before the multiple plane
To look more ways than left and right,
And weeping walks its father's house
Like something homeless in the night:
For now less largely let abroad,
Though but the world they say is mine,
I shiver as I take the road.

Winter Solstice

December, mortal season, crusts
The dark snows shuffled in the street,
And rims the lamp with sleet.
The beggar, houseless, chill, and thin,
Leans to the chestnut vendor's coals,
The cart creaks off which trails the winter bush,
And the thick night shuts in.

Prepare the sun his bier,
The sun, the fallen year,
With all the spoil it yields,
For our fresh almanac is shrunk and dry.
Those pheasants whose proud tread
Made royal summer fields
Hang speckled crop to crop,
And swung before the steamy shop
The hare stares out with frozen eye.

O festival most rich,
Converting dead times green,
Which from bare forests plucks
The circumspect bright bush
That burnt among the boughs blackened and thinned,
The staunch unwithered leaf that none had seen
Before both leaf and burr were trodden down,
And the wild summer streamed upon the wind.

The sun declines in pride,
The year draws underground,
With much beside;

And flesh which has survived,
Outlived its times' defeat,
Rides now the skeleton,
Secure by what is gone,
To taste a pious meat.
How should that other praise,
Whose loss will not corrupt,
The triumph of its days?
Why this—that had
Not more than breath in mind—
The mortal, feasts unblanched
Among a dying kind.
Then, spirit, if you must
Give a more lasting forfeit than a dust
Which owes but to the West,
Reflect, a more entire estate
Is of such charge possessed,
And lordly calendars its progress show;
For that sun's course which measured the extent
Of so much treasurable worth
Saw your goods tried, not spent.
You scorned to hold of time, and so
Get not time's rate,
But sign alone
The payment without date.
Its little tithe has cost the dust as dear,
That, ringed with death,
Makes its own mock in this late wreath,
A twelvemonth green, and in the binding sere.

Those Not Elect

Never, being damned, see paradise.
The heart will sweeten at its look;
Nor hell was known, till paradise
Our senses shook.

Never hear angels at laughter,
For how comports with grief to know
Wisdom in heaven bends to laughter, laughter,
Laughter upon woe?

Never fall dreaming on celestials,
Lest, bound in a ruinous place,
You turn to wander with celestials
Down holy space.

Never taste that fruit with the soul
Whereof the body may not eat,
Lest flesh at length lay waste the soul
In its sick heat.

Quiet

Since I took quiet to my breast
My heart lies in me, heavier
Than stone sunk fast in sluggish sand,
That the sea's self may never stir,
When she sweeps hungrily to land,
Since I took quiet to my breast.

Strange quiet, when I made thee guest,
My heart had countless strings to fret
Under a least wind's fingering.
How could I know I would forget
To catch breath at a gull's curved wing,
Strange quiet, when I made thee guest?

Thou, quiet, hast no gift of rest.
The pain that at thy healing fled
More dear was to my heart than pride.
Now for its loss my heart is dead,
And I keep horrid watch beside.
Thou, quiet, hast no gift of rest.

Thought's End

I'd watched the hills drink the last colour of light,
All shapes grow bright and wane on the pale air,
Till down the traitorous east there came the night
And swept the circle of my seeing bare;
Its intimate beauty like a wanton's veil
Tore from the void as from an empty face.
I felt at being's rim all being fail,
And my one body pitted against space.
O heart more frightened than a wild bird's wings
Beating at green, now is no fiery mark
Left on the quiet nothingness of things.
Be self no more against the flooding dark;
There thousandwise, sown in that cloudy blot,
Stars that are worlds look out and see you not.

A Wind of Fall

A wind went forth a little after dawn,
And sounded his thin horn above the trees,
And there was sudden stilling of those bells
On which the treetoads rang quaint harmonies.

The languid mists upon the morning hills
Melted beneath the wind's swift icy breath;
Each tree took on a loveliness more keen
To taste the rare, bright atmosphere of death.

Each leaf was as a gallant banner flown
For that far runner the wind heralded.
Would they not know the outflung delicate locks
Down all the ways the silver-limbed had fled?

Before the joy of that clear visioning
They had no sorrow, leaf and leaf, to part.
I cry the wind from out the clouds to blow
Through all the dusty summer of my heart.

Rebellion shook an ancient dust,
And bones, bleached dry of rottenness,
Said: Heart, be bitter still, nor trust
The earth, the sky, in their bright dress.

Heart, heart, dost thou not break to know
This anguish thou wilt bear alone?
We sang of it an age ago,
And traced it dimly upon stone.

With all the drifting race of men
Thou also art begot to mourn
That she is crucified again,
The lonely Beauty yet unborn.

And if thou dreamest to have won
Some touch of her in permanence,
'Tis the old cheating of the sun,
The intricate lovely play of sense.

Be bitter still, remember how
Four petals, when a little breath
Of wind made stir the pear-tree bough,
Blew delicately down to death.

An Old Spell

Hearts may not bend in course, but toward its loves,
Through heaping time, shall run the simple river;
And that enchantment that I lightly took
Out of the lovely April is for ever.

O falsely hearing, since of lying tunes,
Three notes were solitary, three apart,
That made of all the insolent armor wax,
Sank in the breast, and pierced the sensible heart;

And eyes forsworn, that, busied with your cheats,
Were fixed with tears, is not that only need,
Beauty's, the desolate wanderer of waste earth,
The sower in darkness of an exquisite seed?

These dropped like dew upon a dreaming flower
That in my breast stirred with delicious morn,
And breathed upon its colour the bleak air,
And felt along its lovely side the thorn.

Not now will I turn from comfortless love again,
Nor, heart, forget the burden that you hold,
And flesh, though it harry you unto the last,
Go ridden through darkness to an end of gold.

City of many, two in deep heaven are shown;
Two pearl, two ivory, two brimful light:
The lifting spire, and the spellworking moon,
That weaves in silver the blue airs of night.
The streets are too live-lustre for her look,
The perished moon's that moves kissing the dead;
But this that the passion and the flesh forsook—
Mary the rose, and the archangels fled—
Is like unshrouded bones, the austere grace
Which, after the worms, its incorruption found.
O strange mortmain! that living have no place,
But that the dead are shuffled underground.
Earth is our mother, whose corrosive bed
From death to dust woos the disdaining dead.

Homecoming

When I stepped homeward to my hill,
Dusk went before with quiet tread;
The bare laced branches of the trees
Were as a mist about its head.

Upon its leaf-brown breast the rocks
Like great grey sheep lay silentwise;
Between the birch trees' gleaming arms
The faint stars trembled in the skies.

The white brook met me halfway down,
And laughed as one that knew me well,
To whose more clear than crystal voice
The frost had joined a crystal spell.

The skies lay like pale-watered deep;
Dusk ran before me to its strand;
And cloudily leaned forth to touch
The moon's slow wonder with her hand.

Merry Month of May

Not the disembodied ones
Are spectres damnèd unto May.
For in and out of buried bones
Wind her roots the colour of death;
For her petals, callow-gay,
Chill is in their dainty breath.

You that died, not false to her,
To a willow-chorus trim,
Shrink not for your mildew air,
Your dank turf locks, to print again
Her bosom—did but eyes grow dim,
The cheeks' roses—only—wane.

Nights that all night long are blue,
Days that the large stars fold in,
She binds her creatures to be true;
Then if flesh be fed and fine,
But those chords snapt, she cries on Sin,
And seals the sky with holy sign.

Midsummer

This starbreak is celestial air
Just silver; earthlight, dying amber.
Underneath an arch of pallor
Summer keeps her brightened chamber.

Bright beauty of the risen dust
And deep flood-mark of beauty pressed
Up from earth in lovely flower,
High against my lonely breast;

Only before the waters fall
Is Paradise shore for gaining now.
The grasses drink the berry-bright dew;
The small fruits jewel all the bough.

Heartbreaking summer beyond taste,
Ripeness and frost are soon to know;
But might such color hold the west,
And time, and time, be honey-slow!

A *Gull Goes Up*

Gulls when they fly move in a liquid arc,
Still head, and wings that bend above the breast,
Covering its glitter with a cloak of dark,
Gulls fly. So as at last toward balm and rest,
Remembering wings, the desperate leave their earth,
Bear from their earth what there was ruinous-crossed,
Peace from distress, and love from nothing-worth,
Fast at the heart, its jewels of dear cost.
Gulls go up hushed to that entrancing flight,
With never a feather of all the body stirred.
So in an air less rare than longing might
The dream of flying lift a marble bird.
Desire it is that flies; then wings are freight
That only bear the feathered heart no weight.

Death and the Lady

Death to the Lady said,
While she to dancing-measure still
Would move, while beauties on her lay,
Simply as dews the buds will fill,
Death said, "Stay!
Tell me, Lady,
If in your breast the lively breath
May flicker for a little space,
What ransom will you give to Death,
Lady?" he said.
"Oh not one joy, oh not one grace,
And what is your will to my will?
I can outwit parched fancies still,"
To Death said the Lady.

Death to that Lady said,
When blood went numb and wearily,
"In innocency dear breath you drew,
And marrow and bloom you rendered me."
She said, "True."
"How now, Lady?"
"My heart sucked up its sweet at will,
Whose scent, when substance' sweet is past,
Is fragrant still, is fragrant still,
Death," she said.
"For bones' reprieve the dreams go last.
Soon, soon, your flowery show must part,
But preciously I cull the heart,"
Death said to the Lady.

Death to that Lady said,
"Is then not all our bargain done?
Or why do you beckon me so fast,
To chaffer for a skeleton
Flesh must cast,
Ghostly lady?"
"For, Death, that I would have you drain
From my dead heart the blood that stands
So chilly in the withered vein;
And, Death," she said,
"Give my due bones into your hands."
"Beauties I claim at morning-prime,
But the lack-lustre in good time,"
Death said to the Lady.

Turning within the body, the ghostly part
Said, *When at last dissembling flesh is riven,*
A little instant when the flesh is cast,
Then thou most poor, steadfast, defeated heart,
Thou wilt stay dissolution, thou thus shriven,
And we be known at last.

This holy vision there shall be:
The desolate breast, the pinioned bird that sings;
The breast-bones whited ivory,
The bird more fair than phoenix-wings.
And hurt, more politic to shun,
It gentles only by its sighs,
And most on the forbidden one
Drop pity and love from the bird's eyes;
And what lips profit not to speak,
Is silver chords on the bird's beak.

Alas!

At the dream's end the ghostly member said,
Before these walls are rotted, which enmesh
That bird round, is the sweet bird dead.
The swan, they say,
An earthly bird,
Dies all upon a golden breath,
But here is heard
Only the body's rattle against death.
And cried, *No way, no way!*
And beat this way and that upon the flesh.

Prelude Pastoral

We leant upon the bended hill,
Where turf is a sheer drop from heaven;
Each to each earth and sky were given,
And all the pointed grass was still
And drank the light till light brimmed even.

A honey milk its roots distil;
The suckling apples topple down;
Not waste, but wizard boughs, so soon
Cast fruitage little, wry and chill
For feasters by the dainty moon.

And dust to no gross thing gives room,
But only for the piercing grass,
The slender-stemmed, the violets, pass,
The crisping curly clover-bloom,
And all is tiny flowers and grass.

We were too still to track the spring,
But pressed our ears upon a sound
Of waters quickening underground;
And if a lark shook out his wing,
That shadow on your cheek I found.

The morning like a rose began,
Rosy and drowsy grows the day;
Its peace will fold the heart away,
Whose thoughts in nearest pastures ran
Within a bell's call all the day.

Discourse with the Heart

I

You witless heart, that of your several beats
So braggart spend, die in a heavenly dream,
And own not any tainting of your sweets;
But in a spring immortal as you seem
Dip that you cherish; O inveterate heart,
You are too wilful to be born again,
Yield the spoilt garner up, and naked start.
Wisdoms shrink off like husks, but loves remain.
Not all the measure of the mind can move,
And love-gainsaying laws are lightly sped,
But your rash hold you keep, and for that love,
The instant-gift, these hourly drops are bled.
At heavens else, where death might never glance,
It was your angel took the toll, not chance.

II

Love is that innocent whom wounding thorn
Will never stop while violets might blow,
And they are tender; once was not wisdom born
Of wounds? But love's feet pierced are steadfast so.
Most dreamy, delicate, headlong wanderer,
Whose star is but some glitter-trick of tears,
Sleep, and my heart will fold you not to stir,
Like one left magic-drowsy, till bleak years
Are done, and the round rose-tree breaks in flowers,
And bees that brew such honey bear no stings,
Till death without, like happy birds the hours,

Like birds, are caged in gold, and yet have wings.
Too docile princess! Love breaks sleep by this,
Each instant starting for the enchanted kiss.

III

Grieved hearts alone to lovers' hearts are kin,
That for no ransom brooded things forego.
If for queen's proudness one be sorrow's twin,
Or one like her disdaining, love is so.
Since now most precious mines can give no gold
So absolute but it's made metaphor,
And richer metal by its shining told,
Nor best, nor beautiful, now the rapt love stir:
Heart, that have loved, nor known it holy part,
(Truth is, live hearts must love as lips shall breathe)
By this shall lift with sanctifying art
Your act of life, who live but to bequeath;
As lips that countless, graceless times have fed,
Save themselves hungry, and bite blessèd bread.

Thief of Paradise

The heart that flowers in the side
Runs from a forbidden root,
And all the best the bosom bears
Is stolen fruit.

One was heard that told of love,
Blest mercy and ease.
But many and ruinous are the tongues,
And cry on these.

You have clasped a mortal liking,
And your bright glance bent on night,
Therefore stolen what was Time's,
Therefore have looked in despite.

How are you seeking love,
Being pointed to hate?
Or how given the wild gait of angels,
You haughty and desperate?

Companions of the Morass

I have seen also your angel,
In the isolation where we had descended
To frequent the naked heart.
Many a time a dove from the thorny branches,
And now one dewy, feathery, tender,
From your eyes will start.

The earth is heavy, and the clouds drop rime,
And night descends without stars;
What does it see, white creature, what do you see, O eyes?
For so at the innocent lady's feet
The blond, the young, delicate ones of heaven,
Stare on the pretty, painted skies.

It is a ground getting demons, but we call no honest demon,
We cannot conjure the swart breed;
The brooding devil at our heels has trod,
But it is he, lord of the circumscribed pit.
Here where holy and unholy are as weak as water,
We encounter the damned god.

It is said, by pinioning the angels
They keep the terrible footway; it is said,
The hardy have traversed the morass,
They that cast out devils to live without sin;
But we, coming between the devil ashamed
And a strayed angel, shall not pass.

How shall we forsake this angel and this devil?
You bottomless tarnished lustre,
And bosom pressed upon the hollow cloud,
How do you visit us, symbols without body?
We are weak earth, we run before the wind
By which our hearts were bowed.

Pity of the Heavens

Light all day from heaven was streaming,
But the last hour gathered earth with light,
Steeping the darkened air with a blue colour;
And now the stars from the lofty brow of the night
Regard the earth, regard the withering land;
And now fair snow comes dropping over her bosom,
Sky touching earth with a chaste hand.

Earth bears no more the print of her creatures' feet;
Dark breast, no more the glittering waters start;
The hare and the doe are uncherished in the wood;
She is numb, there is bitter armor on her heart.

But how profoundly would the heavens caress her,
With pity that hardly is reckoned from eye to eye,
And mouth on mouth is untold.
The amity of the skies has left their touch
So light, so pure, so cold.

O bosom carven upon the roses and pleasures,
Heaven cannot unlock your passions and your mirth,
But have you not perceived those eyes, mournful and bright,
How you are cherished by the countenance of the skies;
Is it not much, O earth?

Now moony light
The dews drink over the black turf;
And earth, at bottom darkness lying,
Looks up on heaven and heavenly night;
Stares on the glittering lady climbing
Her airy arch away,
Till a cold humour of her breast
Infests her clay.

The huntress of the air lets fly,
The beast of earth receives her arrow,
And by those silver arrows maimed,
The bones course with watery marrow.

Now fever-bright the dead moon goes,
The mistress to the sun, that crept
From starveling death, and on his breath
Has fed her lustre while her lover slept.

For the swart earth has breeded of her loves,
But the moon spent upon her withered shell;
And though the moon is barren, she's not cursed,
Nor the fruit unholy to be beautiful.

The stars were scattered at the edge of even,
Clouds may not snare her glittering heels tonight,
And still the amorous gold sun is sleeping,
The earth lies moored, she mounts the brink of heaven.

Night of Unshed Tears

Skies have been bound with such pent airs.
The moon, that mad for brightness stares
Off the black bitter peak of night,
That purest curving crystal even,
Which wasted to a horn trails light,
Moves veiled and brooding over heaven,
With cloud like heavy waters flowing,
And every burnished star sunk deep.
But though the heavens be proud, they weep.
The heaven has wept and thou hast known
Orion, the round liquid moon,
And all washt brightness showing.

The Barouche

Squares south the play was done:
Thick the housetops rise,
Hemming them; all their way
Northerly lies.

Drenched in sleep the cabman,
Drowsy-heeled the mare;
And half in sleep and dreaming,
Travel the fare.

Mournfully, sweetly so,
Midnight to morning goes,
When air has its honey
Of the lilac and rose.

Town is a blackened pool
Hooded with sleep;
And hooves are like bells
With night so deep.

Down every alley corner
Are heavenly gaps laid bare;
They see the clouds driving,
The moon runs there.

Their moon of warmest dusks,
And wasting in late skies,
Who now with perishing
Last silver flies.

If he'd a penny given,
For the mare sweet hay,
And they'd but faith
To be merry that way!

The room is warm, the faces dream.
Out of each hushed and separate sense
Lips will drop words whose difference
No sharper on that air may seem,
Than margin flowers' variance,
That float and drown on one sweet stream.

The wax drops petals of ivory,
Delicate from a waxy swirl,
Smoke and the little trimmed fire curl;
Light for an inch runs amberly.
A lady with a rope of pearl,
Laughs, laughs and laughs and sips her tea.

Above her brows are curveted
Two dainty birds set beak to beak,
Two singing birds whose breasts are sleek.
Her hand, on which she leant her head,
Has left a rose upon her cheek.
Perhaps her birds will sing, though dead.

It is a spell that shuts us so,
Nor breaks so soon that we must see
Bleak light upon the wasted tree;
No, I was learned in spells, to know:
Now on dark wounds falls dreamily,
Like a celestial dew, the snow.

By cold the moon was purged to be
Fairest of stars, and healing so,
Like frost, earth's boughs in March shall blow.
We may not stir till, after tea,
The moon is there, and earth for snow,
As white, as luminous, as she.

Cease to preen, O shining pigeons!
A jewel eye and breast of quiet,
Rainbow neck, will purchase here
Never nest nor wholesome diet.

What would these with muck and soot?
Or to what mortal use bestead
Dainty steppings and a foot
Coral-pink and ringleted?

Did you look, O airish flock,
Now when only breath comes cheap,
For one dirty drudging dock
Seven exquisites to keep?

Pigeons, then you have not known
How Beauty that the waters bred
Creeps up battered and alone
To precarious cup and bread.

Beauty's self, your holy mother,
Here sits not to a goddess' share.
She must live like any other
With no way but being fair.

Stealing up the morning alleys,
And who to tell she is not fraud?
Mortals now are grimly pressed,
That make Beauty to a bawd.

Twilight of the Wood

Leaf is no more now than corruption's scent
But beautiful are the trees above their dead,
This hour with their summer beauties spent,
When desolate of the thousand sweets they shed,
As to that last and western rite made bare, .
Their boughs let drop the amber-yielding cup
That leaves no stain upon the crystal air;
And thinly in their midst a tune goes up:
Then who might sing in all the muted wood?
Its waters locked, no single bird, no leaf;
It is not higher than the living blood
Will sound in bodies stony-dull with grief;
And thus, when death has taken all the rest,
Life's self is heard within earth's icy breast.

Index of POEMS and *First lines*

· 127 ·